T0130223

Hannah:
Woman of Worship

AN INTERACTIVE BIBLE STUDY FOR WOMEN

Karen Morgan

WESTBOW
PRESS®
A DIVISION OF THOMAS NELSON
& ZONDERVAN

Copyright © 2019 Karen Morgan.
Visit our website at wayneandkaren.com.

All rights reserved. No part of this book may be used or reproduced by any means,
graphic, electronic, or mechanical, including photocopying, recording, taping or by
any information storage retrieval system without the written permission of the author
except in the case of brief quotations embodied in critical articles and reviews.

This book is a work of non-fiction. Unless otherwise noted, the author and the publisher
make no explicit guarantees as to the accuracy of the information contained in this book
and in some cases, names of people and places have been altered to protect their privacy.

WestBow Press books may be ordered through booksellers or by contacting:

WestBow Press
A Division of Thomas Nelson & Zondervan
1663 Liberty Drive
Bloomington, IN 47403
www.westbowpress.com
1 (866) 928-1240

Because of the dynamic nature of the Internet, any web addresses or links contained
in this book may have changed since publication and may no longer be valid. The views
expressed in this work are solely those of the author and do not necessarily reflect the
views of the publisher, and the publisher hereby disclaims any responsibility for them.

Unless marked otherwise, all Scripture quotations are taken from The Holy
Bible, English Standard Version® (ESV®), Copyright © 2001 by Crossway,
a publishing ministry of Good News Publishers. All rights reserved.

Scripture quotations marked NIV are taken from The Holy Bible, New
International Version®, NIV® Copyright © 1973, 1978, 1984, 2011 by
Biblica, Inc.® Used by permission. All rights reserved worldwide.

Scripture quotations marked Interlinear Bible are taken from The Interlinear Bible:
Hebrew-Greek-English. Hendrickson Publishers, 1986. Used by permission.

Cover photo by Leeann Manzoni
Cover model Sara Wise
Cover design by Lauren Hodne
Author photo by Melissa Vosburgh

ISBN: 978-1-9736-6913-5 (sc)
ISBN: 978-1-9736-6912-8 (hc)
ISBN: 978-1-9736-6914-2 (e)

Library of Congress Control Number: 2019910163

Print information available on the last page.

WestBow Press rev. date: 10/10/2019

This book is dedicated
with love
to
mi Querida,
my "Beloved Hope,"
my one and only daughter.

Out of all the things
this mother prays for you,
the overarching one is
that you would become
a Woman of Worship.

My heart exults in the Lord ...
I rejoice in your salvation.
There is none holy like the Lord:
for there is none besides you;
there is no rock like our God.

—Hannah
ca. 1100 BC
as recorded in 1 Samuel 2:1–2

My heart exults in the Lord ...
I rejoice in your salvation.
There is none holy like the Lord:
for there is none besides you;
there is no rock like our God.

—Hannah
ca. 1100 BC
as recorded in 1 Samuel 2:1–2

Contents

Introduction

...those who were hungry are hungry no more.
—1 Samuel 2:5 NIV

How to Use This Book

This book has been designed for both personal and group Bible study.

Option 1

For daily personal use, this book provides one month of in-depth Bible study focusing on concepts presented through chapters 1 and 2 of 1 Samuel. Simply do one lesson per day. Some Life Lessons (or chapters) are easily completed in a single daily dose. Other themes take much longer to thoroughly understand and will require several days of study. I had in mind the busy mom of young children when I was dividing up the material. Consequently, I broke down the meatier Life Lessons into more bite-sized pieces that should take about fifteen minutes to complete. These are found in brackets—for example, [Day 1]. To retain the flow as much as possible, I did not break up the larger Life Lessons from Hannah (all of which begin with "Woman of ...") any more than that. If you finish one of the small daily lessons per day (and take Sundays off from personal study), you will finish this Bible study workbook in one month. If you have more time to devote to study (and no small children around your ankles), see option 3.

Option 2

For group study, this book will provide you with six months of lessons for a weekly meeting such as a ladies' Sunday school where the session lasts an hour or less. Each participant should have a copy of the book and work through the lessons on her own at home and then meet with the group to share what God has taught her with other women. For this plan, the goal would be to try to finish one daily lesson at each weekly meeting. This schedule is easily adapted for a group that meets midweek throughout the school year, taking time off for holiday breaks. This should provide you with approximately one school year's worth of material along with ample time for discussion.

As another option for group study, consider doing one Life Lesson from Hannah each week. There are ten Life Lessons, so you may want to schedule about twelve weeks to cover the material with this style of study. This would consist of an introductory week at the beginning, ten weeks of study, and a closing session in which women can practice sharing their stories as an act of worship at the conclusion of the study. There will be a large amount of material to cover some weeks, so this is ideal only if your group meets for well over an hour each time.

Option 3

Of course, you should always work through Bible study material at whatever pace the Lord leads you! Feel free to finish one theme (one chapter) per day or take a whole year to finish the book. The important thing is that we are listening as God is speaking. Psalm 81:10 says, "Open your mouth wide, and I will fill it." Hannah herself said, "Those who were hungry have ceased to hunger" (1 Samuel 2:5). Throughout scripture, God provides both physical and spiritual food for His children. When we come to Him expecting to be fed, He is faithful to bring the provision.

Answering the Questions

The questions asked throughout this book, as well as the suggested scripture passages outside of 1 Samuel, are meant to help you digest God's Word on your own. Please do not get hung up on trying to figure out the "right answer" or "wrong answer." The questions are designed to help you think through things, not for you to fill in all the "right" answers. Because of this, you will not find an answer key in this book. I simply ask you to let God speak to you through His Word. Ask Him what a true and honest answer would be for each question. Expose your heart to Him, and let Him show you what is in it so that He might use this study to transform you more into the image of His Son.

I hope you enjoy your journey.

Karen Morgan

Disclaimer: "It's Not about a Baby"

Many people think the biblical account of Hannah is about a baby. I would argue that it is about much more than that. This true account is about the human heart. It is about an emotional and spiritual journey. It is about the shared human experience of processing a longing or desire. Hannah's longing was indeed for a baby. However, the lessons she has to teach us transcend that single sphere and carry over into any unmet desire you may be experiencing. Like Eli, my hope is that the God of Israel would grant you whatever it is that you have asked of Him. I caution you, though, that in the course of this study, you may find that what you ask of Him begins to change.

Read Proverbs 16:2–3. What is our human tendency in how we view our own goals and desires?

Why do you think it is necessary to commit our plans to the Lord?

Look up Psalm 37:4–5. What does God *want* to give us?

What action on our part must come first?

Throughout this book, you may notice that I refer to Hannah's *story*. Please do not assume that I mean that her story is fictitious. I use the word *story* to encompass a person's entire experience—their encounters and their legacy. It is the narrative of the whole person. I believe Hannah was a real woman who lived in a real place at a real time in history, approximately three thousand years ago. I believe she had valuable thoughts, experiences, emotions, and encounters with God from which we can still learn today. And I intend to take her story apart piece by piece alongside you so that we can dig deeply into scripture and learn from her.

Before I Begin, You Must Begin

Every new chapter of this book is a Life Lesson from Hannah and begins with these words: "Before I begin, you must begin." It is my way of exposing you to the scripture and letting God speak directly to you before I start talking to you at all. Each chapter opens with several scripture verses telling one small piece of Hannah's story, followed by an open-ended question to give you the opportunity to hear directly from God *before* I tell you what He has taught me about that topic. Before we break down Hannah's story piece by piece, we need an overall understanding of who she was.

Take a few moments to write down what you know about Hannah. What is your current understanding of this ancient woman?

It is my prayer that by the time you finish working through this Bible study, you will have a much more thorough concept of the biblical, historical person of Hannah, and that you will believe with your whole heart that her true story has something to teach modern women today. It is my prayer that as we dig into her story, seeking nuggets of truth, the Spirit of God will be unhindered as He works in you to create a Woman of Worship, regardless of your age, your social status, your income, your life situation ... or your longings.

We're going to study just a few pieces of Hannah's story during each Life Lesson, but before we can do that, you need an overall view of who she was and what was going on in her life. So I want you to take several moments to read most of 1 Samuel 1 and 2. Time spent reading God's Word is *never* wasted. As you read, ask the Lord to show you what He has for you in this passage. I've studied it at length, and I seem to find new gems every time I read it, so ask God what He wants you to come away with as you work through this study of Hannah.

As you read, forget for a moment that Hannah is an Old Testament woman who lived three thousand years ago. Rather, consider her a long-lost friend. Picture yourself being caught up on what's been going on in the life of your friend Hannah over the past few years. What would you feel as you heard of her heartache? What questions would you ask that are not addressed in the biblical account? What would you think of her husband? Can you empathize with her roller-coaster of emotions? Think about these things as you read all of 1 Samuel chapter 1, as well as 1 Samuel 2:1–11 and 18–21.

I prefer that you read it from your own Bible (and make tons of notes in it), but I have provided it here in case that is easier for you. *Please don't skip this assignment.* I promise this first reading assignment is the longest one I will ask you to do in this entire book. However, I believe it will be worth it for you. It is imperative that before I start "talking" to you, we allow God to talk to you.

Hannah's Story
1 Samuel 1

There was a certain man ...whose name was Elkanah.... He had two wives. The name of one was Hannah, and the name of the other, Peninnah. And Peninnah had children, but Hannah had no children.

Now this man used to go up year by year from his city to worship and to sacrifice to the Lord of hosts at Shiloh, where the two sons of Eli, Hophni and Phinehas, were priests of the Lord. On the day when Elkanah sacrificed, he would give portions to Peninnah his wife and to all her sons and daughters. But to Hannah he gave a double portion, because he loved her, though the Lord had closed her womb. And her rival used to provoke her grievously to irritate her, because the Lord had closed her womb. So it went on year by year. As often as she went up to the house of the Lord, she used to provoke her. Therefore Hannah wept and would not eat. And Elkanah, her husband, said to her, "Hannah, why do you weep? And why do you not eat? And why is your heart sad? Am I not more to you than ten sons?"

After they had eaten and drunk in Shiloh, Hannah rose. Now Eli the priest was sitting on the seat beside the doorpost of the temple of the Lord. She was deeply distressed and prayed to the Lord and wept bitterly. And she vowed a vow and said, "O Lord of hosts, if you will indeed look on the affliction of your servant and remember me and not forget your servant, but will give to your servant a son, then I will give him to the Lord all the days of his life, and no razor shall touch his head."

As she continued praying before the Lord, Eli observed her mouth. Hannah was speaking in her heart; only her lips moved, and her voice was not heard. Therefore Eli took her to be a drunken woman. And Eli said to her, "How long will you go on being drunk? Put your wine away from you." But Hannah answered, "No, my lord, I am a woman troubled in spirit. I have drunk neither wine nor strong drink, but I have been pouring out my soul before the Lord. Do not regard your servant as a worthless woman, for all along I have been speaking out of my great anxiety and vexation." Then Eli answered, "Go in peace, and the God of Israel grant your petition that you have made to him." And she said, "Let your servant find favor in your eyes." Then the woman went her way and ate, and her face was no longer sad.

They rose early in the morning and worshiped before the Lord; then they went back to their house at Ramah. And Elkanah knew Hannah his wife, and the Lord remembered her. And in due time Hannah conceived and bore a son, and she called his name Samuel, for she said, "I have asked for him from the Lord."

The man Elkanah and all his house went up to offer to the Lord the yearly sacrifice and to pay his vow. But Hannah did not go up, for she said to her husband, "As soon as the child is weaned, I will bring him, so that he may appear in the presence of the Lord and dwell there forever."

Elkanah her husband said to her, "Do what seems best to you; wait until you have weaned him; only, may the Lord establish his word." So the woman remained and nursed her son until she weaned him. And when she had weaned him, she took him up with her, along with a three-year-old bull, an ephah of flour, and a skin of wine, and she brought him to the house of the Lord at Shiloh. And the child was young. Then they slaughtered the bull, and they brought the child to Eli. And she said, "Oh, my lord! As you live, my lord, I am the woman who was standing here in your presence, praying to the Lord. For this child I prayed, and the Lord has granted me my petition that I made to him. Therefore I have lent him to the Lord. As long as he lives, he is lent to the Lord."

And he worshiped the Lord there.

1 Samuel 2:1–11

And Hannah prayed and said,

My heart exults in the Lord;
my horn is exalted in the Lord.
My mouth derides my enemies,
because I rejoice in your salvation.
There is none holy like the Lord:
for there is none besides you;
there is no rock like our God.
Talk no more so very proudly,
let not arrogance come from your mouth;
for the Lord is a God of knowledge,
and by him actions are weighed.
The bows of the mighty are broken,
but the feeble bind on strength.
Those who were full have hired themselves out for
bread,
but those who were hungry have ceased to hunger.
The barren has borne seven,
but she who has many children is forlorn.
The Lord kills and brings to life;
he brings down to Sheol and raises up.
The Lord makes poor and makes rich;

he brings low and he exalts.
He raises up the poor from the dust;
he lifts the needy from the ash heap
to make them sit with princes
and inherit a seat of honor.
For the pillars of the earth are the Lord's,
and on them he has set the world.
He will guard the feet of his faithful ones,
but the wicked shall be cut off in darkness,
for not by might shall a man prevail.
The adversaries of the Lord shall be broken to pieces;
against them he will thunder in heaven.
The Lord will judge the ends of the earth;
he will give strength to his king
and exalt the horn of his anointed.

Then Elkanah went home to Ramah. And the boy was ministering to the Lord in the presence of Eli the priest.

1 Samuel 2:18–21

Samuel was ministering before the Lord, a boy clothed with a linen ephod. And his mother used to make for him a little robe and take it to him each year when she went up with her husband to offer the yearly sacrifice. Then Eli would bless Elkanah and his wife, and say, "May the Lord give you children by this woman for the petition she asked of the Lord." So then they would return to their home.

Indeed the Lord visited Hannah, and she conceived and bore three sons and two daughters. And the boy Samuel grew in the presence of the Lord.

Questions

Does anything strike you about Hannah's story?

Is there a question you are hoping will be answered or something you hope to learn during this Bible study?

What do you think God wants to teach you as you take an intense look at Hannah's life?

Prayer Time

Ask God to reveal to you the area of your life that He is asking you to commit to His plan today. (Consider what you learned when you read Psalm 37:4–5 and Proverbs 16:2–3.)

Thank God for His Word and its power. *Thank God* for the lives of believers like Hannah who went before us and left us their real-life examples from which we can learn.

Life Lessons from Hannah

Woman of Want

Peninnah had children, but Hannah had none.
—1 Samuel 1:2b NIV

Before I Begin, You Must Begin

The Bible passage for this Life Lesson is 1 Samuel 1:1–5. Read it in your own Bible or here:

> There was a certain man ... whose name was Elkanah ... He had two wives. The name of the one was Hannah, and the name of the other, Peninnah. And Peninnah had children, but Hannah had no children.
>
> Now this man used to go up year by year from his city to worship and to sacrifice to the Lord of hosts at Shiloh, where the two sons of Eli, Hophni and Phinehas, were priests of the Lord. On the day when Elkanah sacrificed, he would give portions to Peninnah his wife and to all her sons and daughters. But to Hannah he gave a double portion, because he loved her, though the Lord had closed her womb.

What do these verses tell us about Hannah? Try to list at least five different pieces of information.

What strikes you as the most important piece of information about her?

I can't help but focus on the ends of verses 2 and 5. The biblical account wastes no time in introducing us to a woman with a great and overwhelming unmet desire. This is why I call Hannah a Woman of Want. She wanted something that she was unable to attain. Don't underestimate the stinging power of those words in verse 2: "Peninnah had children, *but Hannah had no children*" (italics added). Ouch!

I mean, seriously, don't all women dread that terrible feeling of being compared with other women? Is there an area in your life where you feel like it is constantly in your face that you don't measure up? Take a moment to write a prayer to God about that area and how you feel about it. There's power in actually taking the time to identify these areas through written effort, and there is spiritual power when we take those issues to God. (More on that later.)

Now that you've reflected on yourself for a while, let's go back to Hannah's story.

Throughout history, it's been generally understood that most women have an inner longing to be a mother. I realize that it's somewhat out of fashion to say that, but it's reality nonetheless. It's important that we not project our own views or the views of our culture into Hannah's story. We must understand her within her own historical context. And in the ancient world, that maternal desire was much more than just a longing for an emotional connection. A woman's very identity was wrapped up in her ability to bear children. Barrenness was considered a shame. Read Genesis 16:1–2 to find out how Sarai decided to tackle her childlessness. Summarize her plight and her solution to the situation.

According to Genesis 30:1, what would Rachel have preferred to barrenness?

Are you getting a picture of how these ancient women felt about bearing children?

A childless woman had no one to provide for her upon her husband's death. Read Ruth 1:3, 5, 11–13, and 20–21. Summarize Naomi's circumstances and her feelings about a situation which left her with no sons to care for her.

As if all those pressures weren't enough, a man often married additional wives if his first wife bore no children. However, it is important to realize that although polygamy was common in the ancient world and was even occasionally practiced among the Hebrews, it was never sanctioned by God.[1]

Hannah's desire went well beyond wanting a baby to hold. It was a desire to please her husband, find fulfillment, ensure provision, and in fact to secure status as a worthwhile person in the ancient world.

What about you? As we kick off this Bible study together, ask yourself, "What is my longing? What is that thing that I allow to define me because it is *not* my reality?" Is it marriage? A degree? Children or grandchildren? A role within your church? A certain dress size? A six-figure salary or a house in a certain neighborhood? A future you

---

[1] Walvoord and Zuck, 433.

planned for yourself that just hasn't turned into reality? What's the *one thing* that you think would make your life suddenly be okay? In 1 Samuel 1:11, which we will explore in detail later, the NIV Bible gives us another way to describe this. Hannah said to God, "If you will only ..."

What is your *if only*, your heart's desire? What makes you a Woman of Want? I challenge you to identify that for yourself and confess it to the Lord. Some people wear their *if onlys* on their sleeves. Many women want a husband, a higher-paying job, a child, or maybe an empty nest. Others have secret longings no one would ever guess. And maybe we're afraid to acknowledge even to ourselves that lack in our lives, that *one thing* that is consuming us with desire.

If you can't readily identify your one thing, ask the people around you. Your husband, parents, children, friends, or pastor will probably know the one thing that characterizes you as a Woman of Want. Better yet, ask your heavenly Father, who knows the deepest longings of our hearts. And when we ask Him to reveal those longings to us, He is faithful to do so.

As you identify your areas of want, it is important to realize that you are not alone in your longings. Most of us wish something in our lives were different. Check out the following Bible passages and identify what each person wanted. Then write down to whom (or what) the person turned in his or her efforts to get the desire met.

Person and Passage	What the Person Wanted	Where Did the Person Turn?
Paul (2 Corinthians 12:6–8)		
Widow (1 Kings 17:17–24)		
Esther (Esther 4:12–16)		
Naomi (Ruth 1:3, 11–13, 20–21)		
Naaman (2 Kings 5:1, 6, 10–14)		
Jairus (Mark 5:22–23)		
Absalom (2 Samuel 15:4–6 & 10–12)		

Person and Passage	What the Person Wanted	Where Did the Person Turn?
David (2 Samuel 15:13–16)		
Nehemiah (Nehemiah 1:3–4)		
Job (Job 29:1–6, 31:35)		

Look through your chart at the column titled "What the Person Wanted." Circle all the wants that are good and appropriate.

Now look at the column titled "Where Did the Person Turn?" Circle all the examples that are good and appropriate places toward which to turn in a season of want.

Write down your *one thing*. What is the one thing you are longing for?

Person	What I Want	Where Have I Been Turning, Until Today?
Me		

Prayer Time for a Woman of Want

Ask God to help you surrender your want to Him.

Thank God that you are not alone in your longing. Thank Him for biblical and modern-day examples of both positive and negative ways of dealing with your wants.

Life Lessons from Hannah

Woman of Worth

...because he loved her....
—1 Samuel 1:5 NIV

[Day 4]

Before I Begin, You Must Begin

The Bible passage for this Life Lesson is from 1 Samuel 1:4–5 and 8. Read it in your own Bible or here:

> On the day when Elkanah sacrificed, he would give portions to Peninnah his wife and to all her sons and daughters. But to Hannah he gave a double portion, because he loved her, though the Lord had closed her womb.

> And Elkanah, her husband, said to her, "Hannah, why do you weep? And why do you not eat? And why is your heart sad? Am I not more to you than ten sons?"

What do you notice in these verses about Hannah and her relationship with Elkanah?

Do any words jump out at you?

In the previous chapter, I asked you to identify your area of want—the area of your life where you long for resolution. But before we get too melancholy, dwelling on our areas of desperation, I want you to see something incredibly important about Hannah. Did you catch it in verse 5? Elkanah was motivated to treat Hannah with respect out of his love for her. The very next phrase reminds us again that she was barren, but this fact did not stop her husband from showing that he valued her. Even though she bore him no children and he had probably taken a second wife because of her infertility, the scripture says he loved her!

In verse 8, Elkanah tried to comfort Hannah. In our next chapter, we will discuss more about that failed attempt, but here's what I want you to see for today: *He tried!* Elkanah cared about his wife and her feelings: "Hannah, why do you weep? And why do you not eat? And why is your heart sad?"

I believe Hannah was a Woman of Worth. Proverbs 31:10 says, "A wife of noble character who can find? She is *worth far more* than rubies" (NIV, italics added).

Think about it. I know few men who are content to live with a woman who is constantly weeping, downhearted, and refusing to eat. What little we know about this marriage seems to indicate that Elkanah was *not* disappointed in his wife despite her barrenness. He was willing to remain with her and provide for her, and he even shows her favor and compassion. He tries to point out the blessings that they share together. I believe that we are introduced to Hannah during a season of desperation, but that discontentment was not a lifestyle for Hannah. It makes me wonder what she was like. What was her personality? What character traits did she possess that caused her husband to respect her so much? She must have been one incredible lady!

Just for fun, use your imagination and write down why you think Elkanah loved his wife, Hannah. What attributes do you suppose she possessed to cause him to value her so highly?

Now read Proverbs 31:10–31 and take inventory of your own excellence. What character traits do you emulate well? Which ones need work?

What does 1 Peter 3:3–4 teach us about our worth?

An interesting side note: Many translations of Proverbs 31:10 say that the excellent wife is more valuable than *rubies*. One possible translation of the name Peninnah is "coral" or "rubies," whereas the meaning of the name Hannah is "grace" according to Ronald F. Youngblood.[2]

Which kind of woman do you want to be? Do you want to emulate Hannah or Peninnah? Write a prayer to God, asking Him to help you become the type of woman He wants you to be.

---

[2] In Gaebelein, 3:576.

While we contemplate the idea of being a Woman of Worth, we should take note of this interesting fact: Elkanah showed his wife that she was a Woman of Worth *before* her status changed to the one she thought would give her value. She was looking down on herself because she had no children, but the Bible clearly says Elkanah loved her in the midst of her infertility. In the middle of what she perceived as failure and disappointment, her husband showed her favor. I recognize that not all men are like that. In truth, one's worth and value cannot be based even in the best of human relationships. (Keep reading. There is a relationship that surpasses anything this tangible world has to offer.) But I think Elkanah was a wonderful example of Christ in the love that he demonstrated. Hannah's husband did not wait for Hannah to prove herself before he loved her. He loved her even before she valued herself.

Check out the following examples. Write down what these people were called to be. Notice in particular whether these leaders held positions of status at the time of their calling.

Person	Called to be ...	Called to Greatness while ...
David	Acts 13:22–23	1 Samuel 16:6–12
Esther	Esther 2:17; 4:7–8; 8:5–8	Esther 2:2–4, 2:7–8
Saul/Paul	Acts 17:1–4 (This is just one example of Paul's calling.)	Acts 7:55–8:1a Acts 9:1–18

Now look at Romans 5:6–11. When does verse 8 say that Christ poured out His love on us?

Person	Called to be ... (as found in Romans 5:10–11)	Called to this greatness while ... (Romans 5:8)
Me		

God does not wait for us to prove that we are "worthwhile" people before He lavishes His kindness on us. He shows us the greatest demonstration of love while we still have our issues, our problems ... and the evil that truly *does* make us unworthy.

Have you thanked God today for His incomprehensible act of love in showing us value, compassion, and worth even when we have none of our own to offer Him?

While we contemplate the idea of becoming Women of Worth, let me give you another reason why I believe Hannah was a woman of great value: she showed a willingness to be corrected. Reread Elkanah's admonition to her in 1 Samuel 1:8. What did he say about her heart?

Ronald F. Youngblood tells us that the word translated as "sad" in the ESV or "downhearted" in the NIV more literally means, "Why is your heart *bad*?" In Deuteronomy 15:10, we find another use of this phrase.[3] Read Deuteronomy 15:7–10 to find out what the hearer is being asked to do in this passage.

What does the phrase about the heart in Deuteronomy 15:10 teach us about Elkanah's use of this same phrase in 1 Samuel 1:8?

Perhaps more important than Elkanah's precise wording is Hannah's response. Regardless of what happened in that marital interchange, the verses immediately after them tell us that Hannah's response to this conversation was to arise and go to the temple.

What does Proverbs 12:1 tell us that our response should be regarding correction?

Do you typically respond to correction the way that Proverbs 12:1 admonishes us to respond?

---

[3] In Gaebelein, 3:572.

Sneak peek ahead: Check out another example where Hannah is exemplified as a Woman of Worth. Read 1 Samuel 1:21–23, which tells a portion of Hannah's life story that occurred after the birth of Samuel. What do these verses imply about the trust level in Elkanah and Hannah's marriage?

Did Elkanah seem to think that his wife's judgment could be trusted?

Now read Proverbs 31:10–12. You may want to write out verses 11 and 12 below. If you do not have a husband, *please do not assume these words are not for you.* Although this passage is specifically written about wives, the general topic is women and character traits. Regardless of your marital status, there is probably someone who *should* be able to have full confidence in you. Who is affected by your level of trustworthiness? Who bears the repercussions of judgment calls left to your discretion? If not a spouse, is it your parents, employer, employees, friends, relatives, students, those you serve in ministry, fellow church members, or neighbors?

A Word about Areas of Influence

I realize that the passage in 1 Samuel 1:21–23 occurred *after* the birth of Samuel, and perhaps Hannah had matured a lot during the process of praying, pregnancy, and mothering. But chronologically, the example of Hannah's worth from 1 Samuel 1:5 and 8 falls *before* the conception of her child, so it begs the question, What effect did Hannah have on her husband? He clearly cherished her and cared deeply about her heartache. Based on your overview of 1 Samuel 1 and 2, does anything in the biblical account indicate that Peninnah held Elkanah's heart, compassion, or respect in the way that Hannah did?

Hannah longed to mold the heart of a child, but did she realize the influence she may have had on her husband? How often are we guilty of pining for influence in one area while poorly stewarding an area of influence God has already given us?

Many women easily slip into longing for the next phase of life. We long for academic degrees, marriage, promotions and titles at work, and children. Then we long for an empty nest. Many women who must work outside the home long to be *in* the home, and many stay-at-home moms long for the satisfaction and fulfillment of a nine-to-five job, not to mention the paycheck. Some grandmothers long to see their grandkids every single day and watch them grow up. Other grandparents wish they could retire and take a cross-country road trip, but they're too busy getting their grandkids off the bus every day and providing child care. We long for ministry positions that

God has not entrusted to us. The woman whose body is out of shape from multiple pregnancies longs for a streamlined physique, and the woman in the size two dress looks on longingly and wonders if she will ever carry a baby safely to term.

Are we ever satisfied with the realm of influence God has given to us? Ask God if you are guilty of longing for what He has not yet given you while neglecting a sphere of influence in which He has already placed you. If God reveals anything to you in your prayer, write it down here. (You may want to read Philippians 4:10–13.)

In the previous chapter, I asked you to identify what makes you a Woman of Want. Now consider your own worthiness. Are you a Woman of Worth?

So often we fall into the trap of believing that our worth comes from what we have or lack, but our responsibility is to cultivate value from the inside out. Have you pursued the disciplines that will develop you into a woman prized far above precious jewels? Have you gained respect and influence in some area? Are you content with the role God has currently given you? Are you using your influence well?

Prayer Time for a Woman of Worth

Ask God to make you into the woman He wants you to be, a woman of noble character, a Woman of Worth, regardless of your situation.

Ask God to reveal areas where you long for influence that He has not yet given.

Thank God for loving you while you were yet a sinner. Praise Him for not waiting until you reached a certain status level before pouring out His love on you. Thank Him for the areas of influence He has given you.

When we are willing to
surrender our wants *to Him*,
find our worth *in Him*,
and use our sphere of influence *for Him*,
then God is free to accomplish
His purposes in our lives.

Life Lessons from Hannah

Woman of Wounds

...her rival provoked her till she wept and would not eat.
—1 Samuel 1:7b NIV

Before I Begin, You Must Begin

The passage for this Life Lesson is from 1 Samuel 1:2, 6–8, 12–16. Read it in your own Bible or here. (Italics added.)

[Elkanah] had two wives. The name of the one was Hannah, and the name of the other, Peninnah. And Peninnah had children, but Hannah had no children.

*****

And her rival used to provoke her grievously to irritate her, because the Lord had closed her womb. So it went on *year by year.* As often as she went up to the house of the Lord, she *used to provoke her.* Therefore Hannah wept and would not eat. *And Elkanah, her husband, said to her, "Hannah, why do you weep? And why do you not eat? And why is your heart sad? Am I not more to you than ten sons?"*

*****

As she continued praying before the Lord, *Eli observed her mouth.* Hannah was speaking in her heart; only her lips moved, and her voice was not heard. Therefore *Eli took her to be a drunken woman. And Eli said to her, "How long will you go on being drunk? Put your wine away from you."* But Hannah answered, "No, my lord, I am a woman troubled in spirit. I have drunk neither wine nor strong drink, but I have been pouring out my soul before the Lord. Do not regard your servant as a worthless woman, for all along I have been speaking out of my great anxiety and vexation."

What stands out to you in today's passage?

With which person in the account do you most easily identify?

We have already been introduced to the biblical account of Hannah as a Woman of Want and Worth. She was a Woman of Want because she had a great longing, an overwhelming unmet desire. She was a Woman of Worth because the interactions with her husband that are documented in scripture show that he deeply cherished and respected her.

I asked you to use your imagination to fill in the rest of Hannah's character and personality, the parts that are not clearly outlined in scripture. What was this woman like? What attitudes and behaviors would result in a wife being treated so favorably by her husband? You thought through these questions by naming traits from Proverbs 31 and your own experiences.

We noted that Hannah appears to have been cherished by Elkanah even *before* bearing him a son. We explored biblical passages where God called various individuals to greatness while they were in the midst of the mundane. We studied Romans 5:6–10 and found that God called us to be reconciled to himself when we were still in the midst of our sin. (See also 2 Corinthians 5:16–21.)

After that study, you were challenged to consider the spheres where you already have influence, and you were encouraged to steward that influence well. We do not honor God when we waste our time longing for some area of influence that has not yet been granted to us.

I hope you are gaining a better understanding not only of the scriptural person of Hannah, but of the valuable lessons she can teach modern women that cross the span of time and geographical boundaries.

Now I want you to notice something you may have overlooked in your initial reading of Hannah's story. A *want*, which I define as an unmet expectation or desire, is not the same as a *wound*.

Here's how *Webster's New World College Dictionary* defines *wound*: "(1) an injury to the body in which the skin or other tissue is broken, cut, pierced, torn, etc.; (2) an injury to a plant caused by cutting, scraping, or other *external* force; (3) any hurt or injury to the feelings, honor, etc."[4] (Italics added.)

By the way, *Webster's* definition of *want* includes "to be lacking," "to feel the need of, long for, crave," and "a wish or desire for something."[5]

Note: There is an immense difference between a *want* and a *wound*. A *want* is something we feel we are lacking. It's the disappointment of life not really turning out the way we expected—things not going the way we dreamed. A *wound* is much more severe, causing us to feel pierced, crushed, torn, like we are broken in some way.

Did you notice that one definition for *wound* said it was caused by an external force? In my experience, wants are just part of life. You thought you'd get the promotion, but you didn't. You thought you'd

---

4 *Webster's New World College Dictionary*, 4th ed. (2001), s.v. "wound."

5 *Webster's*, s.v. "want."

be married by now, but you're not. You thought somebody at church would finally recognize how gifted you are, but no one has. You thought you'd be proud of your kids, but they disappoint you. You thought that by the time you hit midlife, you wouldn't have to struggle to pay the bills, but you still do. That's a want—a lack, a desire for something.

But all too often the wants of this world are compounded by *wounds*— the greater heartache of the soul that causes us to think internal surgery will be needed before we will ever feel whole again. Did you notice four areas where Hannah's situation of want was compounded by a wound?

First, Hannah suffered the wound of the enemy. In 1 Samuel 1:6–7, how does the Bible refer to Peninnah? What was her role in Hannah's life?

Describe the way Peninnah interacted with Hannah.

How long does this type of interaction last?

Use a dictionary to look up the word your Bible uses to describe Peninnah's relationship to Hannah (*rival, enemy,* etc.). Write the definition below.

What do you think motivated Peninnah to treat Hannah this way?

Second, Hannah may have suffered wounds caused by well-meaning friends and family. Read 1 Samuel 1:8. Would these words have brought you comfort in Hannah's situation?

Hannah responded well to Elkanah's gentle rebuke, but do you suppose anything that he said got under her skin?

What do you think motivated Elkanah to interact with Hannah in this way?

We all know people who genuinely love and care about us, people who would never hurt us on purpose. But sometimes they just don't get it. They cannot fully understand us, and their comments hurt. At the core of it all, what Elkanah had to offer was not what Hannah's soul needed, as is evidenced by the fact that her next move was to go and pray.

Have you ever faced a situation where you were *wanting*, and then you experienced the deeper pain of being *wounded* by an enemy or a well-meaning friend or relative? If so, write about it here.

But wait: there was a third source of wounding for Hannah, and I find it to be the saddest of them all. Hannah was wounded by the religious community. Read 1 Samuel 1:12–16.

Did Eli have a full understanding of Hannah's situation?

Did Eli *assume* that he fully understood the situation?

Of what did Eli accuse Hannah in verse 14?

What do you think motivated Eli to treat Hannah that way?

Look at Hannah's response to Eli in verse 15. How do you think Hannah felt about his accusation?

Hannah, in her wisdom, approached the one place where it was truly appropriate to sort out all her battling emotions. She went to the one place where maybe, just maybe, there would be answers. She went to the only site where she could expect to find real power—some strength surpassing her own. She was seeking safety for her tattered heart, and she sought it at the Lord's house. Hannah went to there to pray—*and she was judged*. Assumptions were made about her, and hurtful words were thrown at her. Her character was maligned. In the one place where her tumultuous emotions should have found refuge, Hannah was met instead with condemnation.

Oh, how I wish this never happened today where the people of God gather. How I wish the representatives of God on this earth were immune to making the same mistake that Eli made, but I cannot truthfully say that. These things still happen today. But make no mistake—if the people of God have hurt you, judged you, condemned you, or thrown accusing words at you, these things did not come from the Father, but just from one sinful heart to another.

[Day 10]

As we further investigate Eli's wrong assumption about Hannah, read Hebrews 5:1–3. How was the priest supposed to interact with the people he served?

What was supposed to motivate the priest to interact in this way? (Look for wording such as *since* or *because of this*.)

Are religious leaders immune from making mistakes and committing sins? (See Romans 3:23 and Hebrews 5:1–3.)

Our God is a God of reconciliation. He has every right to condemn us, but He stands instead to offer forgiveness through the blood of His Son. By His stripes, we are healed. By His blood, the deepest wounds of our hearts can be healed as well. (See Isaiah 53:4–6.)

And that brings me to Hannah's fourth wound ... *Don't underestimate the internal struggle of Hannah's soul.* We are not privy to her thoughts about Almighty God, but she clearly evidenced a belief in the power of her Lord. She begged God to give her a son, so obviously she believed—rightfully so—that such an act would be within His power. *And yet He had not done this.* We are not left to wonder at the cause of Hannah's infertility. Did you catch that?

Read 1 Samuel 1:5–6. The Bible makes sure to tell us *twice* why Hannah had not been given a child, and the Word of God makes no apology for that situation. Who was responsible for Hannah's circumstances?

Do you suppose Hannah had a difficult time reconciling her situation with what she knew to be true of God?

Read 1 Samuel 1:3–4. How often did Hannah and her family make the trip to Shiloh?

Does this indicate that her religious experience would be a major or a minor part of her life?

Wondering about Shiloh? That's where the tabernacle of the Lord was erected, making it the religious center of Israel for more than three hundred years.[6] Apparently, pious Israelites were expected to make an annual pilgrimage there to fulfill vows.[7]

Read Hannah's prayer in 1 Samuel 1:11. Did she believe that God could both *hear* and *answer* prayer?

Taking these factors into consideration, even before the birth of Samuel, Hannah probably had some understanding of God's ability as creator of life, hearer of prayer, and defender of the weak. However, these truths may have been difficult to reconcile with the reality of her own life. She would certainly not have been the first person to feel that way.

---

[6] Kaiser and Garrett, 397.
[7] Kaiser and Garrett, 401.

Summarize what you know about the biblical character of Job. (For some help understanding his situation, go to Job 1:13–19 and 2:7–8.)

Now read Job 30:20–23. How did Job feel in these verses?

Did Job understand the ways of God? Or was it a struggle for him to make sense of the reality of his situation, compared with his knowledge about God?

What does Isaiah 55:8–9 tell us about attempting to rationalize God's work in our lives?

Have you ever had an internal struggle where what you knew of your situation and what you knew to be true of God just didn't seem to match? Have you ever stood before Him saying, "God, I *know* you can do something about this. Why won't You act?" Name that situation below.

Of the areas discussed that can cause us to become Women of Wounds, which one has added the most "insult to injury" in your own life?

We've done a lot of introspection during the last three chapters. Now it's time to look at all of this from another angle. What if we are the person who is *doing the wounding?* Ask God to show you whether you, like Peninnah, have treated someone as the enemy. Write a prayer asking God for His forgiveness. End the prayer by telling Him when and where you commit to reaching out to this person and making the situation right.

Ask God to reveal to you if you, like Elkanah, may have wounded someone by being a friend or relative who is well meaning but just doesn't get it. Write a prayer committing that person to the Lord's care. If you feel led to apologize for anything, *do it today* while the Holy Spirit is pricking your heart.

Ask God to reveal to you whether you, like Eli, have caused wounds while representing the religious community. Write a prayer of confession and ask God to show you how to mend the hurt you have caused.

Allow God to reveal to you whether your heart has wrongfully questioned His sovereign plans for your life. Read what Job says in 40:3–5 after the God of the universe speaks to him. Write those verses below, replacing Job's name with your own.

> "Then [Karen] answered the Lord:
> 'I am unworthy—how can I reply to you?
> I put my hand over my mouth.
> I spoke once, but I have no answer—
> twice, but I will say no more'"
> (Job 40:3–5 NIV).

These verses became so meaningful to me several years ago when my husband received a diagnosis of cancer. He was twenty-six years old, and his cancer was so severe that we were told he was more likely to die before reaching his thirties than to spend those years with me.

Yes, I had questions. Yes, people asked me, "How could a good God let this happen?" No, I did not have any answers. But God led me to those verses from Job, and I knew that sometimes I needed to put my hand over my mouth and stop the words from coming out.

I'm not saying that I often succeeded at following these instructions, but I *am* saying that God is faithful. My place is to be on my knees before Him—not shaking my fist at Him. God is in heaven, and I am on earth. Father, let my words be few. (See Ecclesiastes 5:2.)

Write a prayer if God has shown you any area where you need to put your hand over your mouth and trust His ways.

Prayer Time for a Woman of Wounds

Ask God to bless those who have despitefully used you (Luke 6:28) as well as your well-meaning friends and family, and your religious leadership.

Thank God for the fact that He will never fail you and His ways are always good—even when we do not understand them.

Life Lessons from Hannah

Woman of Wisdom

Hannah stood up.
—1 Samuel 1:9 NIV

Before I Begin, You Must Begin

The Bible passage for this Life Lesson is from 1 Samuel 1:9 and 12a. Read it in your own Bible or here. (Italics added.)

> After they had eaten and drunk in Shiloh, Hannah rose. Now Eli the priest was sitting on the seat beside the doorpost *of the temple of the Lord.*

*****

> As she continued praying *before the Lord....*

What strikes you about Hannah in these two short verses?

Where is Hannah in these verses?

There is no better time than in doubt and sorrow to exercise wisdom. It is not that our questions aren't worth asking, or that our wounds do not matter to the holy, all-powerful One. But what matters even more is *where we go* with our questions, doubts, unmet desire, and wounded hearts. In this, Hannah beautifully exemplifies a Woman of Wisdom. She knows where to go.

Notice that Hannah didn't call her mother and have a good cry. She didn't gossip about Peninnah to another friend, or ask Eli a theological question like, "How could a good God allow my dreams to go unfulfilled?" She did not demand that her husband take care of her problems by becoming hysterical like Rachel of old, who wailed to Jacob, "Give me children or else I die!" (Genesis 30:1).

No, none of these are the response of a truly wise woman. First Samuel 1:9 says that after the sacrificial meal was finished—apparently not by Hannah, who refused to eat according to verse 7—"Hannah stood up" (NIV).

She proceeded to go to the tabernacle, though we are not told why until later. In the next Life Lesson, we will look at the prayer that Hannah prayed. But for now, it's important for us to see *where* she went with all her tattered emotions, longings, hurts, and confusion. She got as close as she could possibly get to the presence of God.

Was she welcome at the tabernacle? The resounding answer is yes! Maybe not by Eli at first, but certainly by her heavenly Father, a God who has been pursuing His people since the dawn of time.

After all, she had no one else to whom she could turn. Hannah probably felt emotions similar to those later described in Psalm 73:25–28. What does the Psalmist say in these verses about his relationship with God and time spent in God's presence?

Fast-forward to the New Testament, when Christ had come to earth to remove any boundaries between us and the Holy One. We no longer have to go to a specific geographical location to be in His presence. We no longer need an earthly priest to make intercession for us. There is no longer any separation between us and the holiest place. We can go straight to the Father, pleading our right to be there by the blood of His son, Jesus. What does 1 Peter 5:7 invite us to do?

In the last Life Lesson, we discussed the fact that even a priest in Hannah's day could make a mistake. He had to have a sacrifice to cover even his own sins. What does Hebrew 4:14–16 teach us about approaching God when we are hurting?

What are your deepest hurts today? Name them here.

Now ask yourself, where do I go when I hurt? Do I bury my wounds in gossip, workaholism, or ice cream? Do I put an undue burden on a good friend, a spouse, a parent, or a child by expecting that person to carry my load? Do I turn to pop culture or my pastor? Or do I model *wisdom* and take my concerns straight to the One who created me and loves me more deeply than anyone else could ever comprehend?

Prayer Time for a Woman of Wisdom

Ask God to help you deal wisely with both your wants and your wounds, by taking them to the appropriate place.

Thank God that He has invited us into His presence, that we can approach His throne of grace with confidence (Hebrews 4:14–16) because of the sacrifice of Jesus (Hebrews 10:19–22).

Life Lessons from Hannah

Woman of Weeping

I was pouring out my soul....
—1 Samuel 1:15 NIV

Before I Begin, You Must Begin

The passage for this Life Lesson is 1 Samuel 1:9–16. Read it in your own Bible or here:

> After they had eaten and drunk in Shiloh, Hannah rose. Now Eli the priest was sitting on the seat beside the doorpost of the temple of the Lord. She was deeply distressed and prayed to the Lord and wept bitterly. And she vowed a vow and said, "O Lord of hosts, if you will indeed look on the affliction of your servant and remember me and not forget your servant, but will give to your servant a son, then I will give him to the Lord all the days of his life, and no razor shall touch his head."
>
> As she continued praying before the Lord, Eli observed her mouth. Hannah was speaking in her heart; only her lips moved, and her voice was not heard. Therefore Eli took her to be a drunken woman. And Eli said to her, "How long will you go on being drunk? Put your wine away from you." But Hannah answered, "No, my lord, I am a woman troubled in spirit. I have drunk neither wine nor strong drink, but I have been pouring out my soul before the Lord. Do not regard your servant as a worthless woman, for all along I have been speaking out of my great anxiety and vexation."

What strikes you most about the way Hannah interacted with God?

Hannah is our example of where to turn with our longings, questions, wounds, and dreams. Our first place of refuge should not be a self-help book, a sister, or a scathing social media post. We should not turn even to a spouse, prayer group, or pastor. We are to take full advantage of our access to the Father and call on His name.

So how do we approach the Father? He answered Hannah's prayer, so maybe we can learn something from her example.

Praying with Tears

This is where I introduce you to Hannah as a Woman of Weeping. What words or phrases in today's passage give us a mental picture of how Hannah presented herself in the temple?

Is it ever okay to cry out in prayer? Read Psalm 42:1–5. Do you see any parallels between this psalm and Hannah's petition?

Tears are not the problem. It's what we do with them that matters—and Hannah did a beautiful thing with her tears, something we would do well to imitate. She took them to the Father. She went to the one place where her emotions, confusion, and frustration should be safe, and she laid it all out before her God.

For further study on crying out to God, complete the following chart:

Passage	What I learned about God and emotions
Psalm 62:8	
Psalm 34:17–18	
Psalm 39:12	
Psalm 17:1	
Psalm 61:1–3	
Psalm 28:2	
Psalm 102:1–2	
Psalm 56:8	

Praying with Honesty

There is an honesty with which Hannah interacted with the sovereign God. She made no pretense. Hannah's prayer "is not formal, contrived, or ritualistic. It is as direct as any might wish it to be."[8] In her honesty before the Creator, I believe she opened the door for Him to perform miracles in her heart.

Taking our emotions to the Lord in a season of sorrow is a good and beautiful thing. Although He may straighten out our thinking as He did with Job, He does not condemn us for bringing those thoughts to Him.

How do we balance the idea that sometimes we need to put our hand over our mouth (Job 40:3–5) with the open invitation in 1 Peter 5:7 to cast all our cares on Him because He cares for us? I don't pretend to have the answer to that question. From my study of the Bible, all I can figure out is that it may depend on the condition and motivations of the heart.

Praying with Humility

Look at 1 Samuel 1:11. In the midst of her pain, on whom did Hannah depend?

What phrase did Hannah use repeatedly to refer to herself in 1 Samuel 1:11?

---

[8] Kaiser et al., 201.

What would be the indications of such a relationship with the most high God? Who is in charge?

Did Hannah believe that God was capable of providing her with a child?

Did Hannah make demands of God, believing she was entitled to God's intervention? Or did she choose to use a conditional statement in this verse? ("If this, then that.")

Kaiser et al. write, "There is no demanding or threatening here [in Hannah's prayer] ... God was not obligated to answer her. But the fact that he did indicates that he judged her motives to be right and her request appropriate."[9]

Praying with Surrender

What promise did Hannah make at the end of 1 Samuel 1:11?

At that point, did Hannah even have the one thing for which she had been longing?

---

[9] Kaiser et al., 201.

What was she willing to do with that one thing if God granted her request?

I look at Hannah's example, and I am forced to ask myself, *When I pray, do I approach God the way Hannah did?*

Do I come to Him in tears, with my soul bared, in deep anguish? He knows my heart anyway, so I may as well voluntarily expose it to Him.

Do I come to Him in humility? Do I understand that He alone can heal both my situation and my tortured heart?

Do I leave it up to Him to decide if—and when—He will act?

Do I come to Him in surrender? Am I ready, before He even gives me what I ask, to turn it all back over to Him in a sacrifice of praise?

It's worth taking some extra time to examine the way we pray when we approach the Father. Could it be that we don't see evidence of the effects of our prayers because we aren't asking the right way, with the right attitude? Read James 4:2b–3. What are some reasons that we do not receive from God what we have requested?

Of course, Jesus Himself is our best example of how to pray through a difficult situation. Read Luke 22:42. What internal battle is Jesus facing? (Continue reading the rest of Luke 22 and all of Luke 23 if you are unfamiliar with the context of this prayer of Jesus. And after that, you may as well go on to read Luke 24:1–12, so you'll know how this all ends!)

If Jesus were looking only at His own comfort, He would never have agreed to the cross. What part of Luke 22:42 alludes to this?

Does Jesus hesitate to tell the Father what He wants?

Does Jesus end His prayer by stating His own desire? Or does He state His wish and then surrender His own desire to the Father's plan? (See also Philippians 2:5–8.)

I am so thankful that Jesus's greatest struggle illustrates two concepts that initially appear to be diametrically opposed to each other: we have the freedom to speak openly to the Father about the desires of our heart, but we also have the obligation to lay those wishes down before His throne in surrender.

What might God do if we asked Him correctly? He's willing to hear us. What doors are you praying for God to open as you approach Him in your weeping, seeking Him with an honest heart full of humility and surrender?

Prayer Time for a Woman of Weeping

Ask God to help you develop a heart full of humility and surrender, a heart that holds loosely to your own plans and desires.

Thank God for the example of Christ Himself, who has experienced every weakness of the flesh, yet given us a sinless example (Hebrews 4:15).

Life Lessons from Hannah

Woman of Waiting

So in the course of time ...
—1 Samuel 1:20a

Before I Begin, You Must Begin

The Bible passage for this Life Lesson is from 1 Samuel 1:17–19a. Read it in your own Bible or here:

> Then Eli answered, "Go in peace, and the God of Israel grant your petition that you have made to him." And she said, "Let your servant find favor in your eyes." Then the woman went her way and ate, and her face was no longer sad. They rose early in the morning and worshiped before the Lord.

Does anything stand out to you in these verses?

This is where I introduce you to Hannah as a Woman of Waiting. This is the in between time, the season of her life that is glossed over in most children's Sunday school curriculums. The prayer had been stated, the petition had been poured out, and now she waited … for an answer.

We tend to think of *waiting* as that thing we do at the doctor's office in the room they so helpfully refer to as "the waiting room." We sit around, bored, feeling awkward, doing nothing, wasting time on our phones. We flip through a magazine that we aren't really interested in, waiting for the real event to get started, the one we really came here for.

But that's not waiting with an eternal perspective. Look up Isaiah 40:31. What waiting (or hoping) are we expected to do?

Geoffrey W. Grogan writes, "The verb used in verse 31a suggests an exchange of strength."[10] Oh, how beautiful it is to exchange my failing, limited strength for God's strength that never runs out!

My favorite verse in Hannah's story could easily be overlooked. Reread 1 Samuel 1:18b, the part *after* she stopped talking. List the three things Hannah did in this verse. The ESV says, "Then the woman ..."

1.

2.

3.

Hannah changed a lot as her story unfolded. Do you recall how we were first introduced to her? Look back at the way Hannah was described in 1 Samuel 1:7, focusing on the end of the verse. What was the status of Hannah's countenance when we first met her?

With what activity did Hannah refuse to be involved in 1 Samuel 1:7?

---

[10] In Gaebelein, 6:246.

Now go back to 1 Samuel 1:18b, where a total transformation had taken place. This was truly a miracle because—don't miss this—what had happened to change Hannah's situation? Absolutely nothing! She walked into that tabernacle not pregnant, and she left the tabernacle not pregnant. And yet something amazing occurred inside that tabernacle—Hannah met with Almighty God! And whatever happened was enough to make her rise from her grief and frustration, change her behavior by eating again, and change her countenance so that her face was no longer sad.

The next verse says they rose up early in the morning—and they worshipped (1:19).

A season of waiting is not an excuse for passivity. It is totally possible to worship God even when it seems that things are not right in your world.

In the last chapter, we learned that it is good and healthy to pour out our hearts before the Lord. He invites us to do so. But we cannot stay in that season of weeping forever. There is a time to come to grips with our situation, dry our tears, and move forward in confidence based on what God has revealed to us during our season of weeping.

Are you in a season of waiting? Have you evaluated your longings and taken your concerns to the Heavenly Father, but it still seems like nothing is happening? Sometimes we pray about a life situation or a broken relationship for decades, and it feels like nothing will ever change. Take a moment to write out a prayer about what you would like to see God do.

Now take a moment to reflect. Assuming that you have poured out your heart before God and accepted His invitation in 1 Peter 5:7, how are you doing at following Hannah's example in 1 Samuel 1:18? Have you set your course, gone on your way, changed your countenance, and changed your behavior? Or are you wallowing in your identity as a Woman of Want and Weeping? Write a prayer asking God to help you wait in a way that honors Him.

This is not meant to be simply a decision where we flippantly say, "I am just not going to worry about it anymore." This is not a denial of the emotion, pain, or loss that the situation brings. Other than Eli's blessing, Hannah had absolutely no evidence that her situation had changed. We often gloss over the waiting periods when we are studying scripture. We need to take a moment to experience the humanity of the situation through which she was persevering as she waited for "in due time" to come.

Hannah saw no evidence that her prayer had been answered, and in fact, there was no possibility of her being pregnant yet. Nevertheless, she rose early in the morning *to worship the Lord* after her time of crying out in the temple. It was not until her family returned home and resumed their normal activities that there could be any hope of pregnancy. (See 1 Samuel 1:19.) True worship has to occur whether or not a given situation has changed. Use your dictionary to write down some definitions of worship.

According to my dictionary, *worship* comes from "worth" plus the suffix "-ship."[11] This would indicate that the word has to do with ascribing to someone the worth (value, merit) that he or she is entitled to receive.

Worship is not to be confused with thanksgiving. We may thank God for what He has done when we feel especially blessed. Perhaps we notice His goodness and generosity to us, and we take the time to say, "Thank you." These are good and appropriate expressions of gratitude, but they do not describe worship at its purest form.

True worship is not based on my satisfaction with what God has handed me in the current events of my life. Rather, it requires that I honor God for who He is, not merely for what He does. And *who He is* remains unchanged by my circumstances here on this earth.

This truth hit home for me several years ago. I woke up one Sunday morning and started getting ready to walk out the door. Now, I'm one of those people who will get a musical phrase stuck in my head and just keep singing it, often not even realizing what the song is. It could be a line from a children's song, a little ditty from a TV commercial, or any number of things.

That Sunday morning, while I put on my makeup in front of the bathroom mirror, I was humming a worship song by Tim Hughes that was popular when I was in college. It goes like this: "Here I am to worship; here I am to bow down. Here I am to say that you're my God."[12]

---

[11] *Webster's New World College Dictionary*, 4th ed. (2001), s.v. "worship."
[12] Hughes.

Suddenly I realized what I was humming. That Sunday morning, I grabbed the sides of the dinky little sink in front of me and stared at myself in the mirror, thinking bitterly, *Yeah, right. Here I am to worship.*

You see, it was Sunday, and I was getting ready to walk out the door, but I was not preparing my family to head to church that day. I did not have the joy of dressing my one-year-old and three-year-old in cute clothes for church because I had left them with my parents weeks earlier. That particular morning, like so many mornings before, I had awakened alone in the Ronald McDonald House of Manhattan.

My plan was to walk five blocks to Sloan Kettering Cancer Center to spend the day by my young husband's side while he fought for his life ... one more day.

A few months earlier, Wayne had received a diagnosis of cancer that had spread from the original site, all the way through his lymph node system, to his liver and lungs. He had already endured surgery to remove the cancer, and in the process he had lost a kidney. When he was only twenty-six years old, my best friend in this entire world had been given a 40 percent chance of survival.

That's what I was facing on that Sunday morning. So when I realized that I was thoughtlessly humming, "Here I am to worship," the irony of my situation was not lost on me.

I wasn't even headed to church that morning, yet I was right where I was supposed to be.

And yes, for a brief moment, I grabbed that sink and thought sarcastically, *Yeah, right. Here I am to worship.*

Thankfully, because so many people were praying for me during that horrendous season, my first bitter thought was quickly replaced by a more appropriate one as I realized,

"Yes, here … *here* I am to worship!

Here in the Ronald McDonald House.

Here as I walk the five blocks to the cancer center.

Here as I try to help make my husband comfortable while his abdomen fills with fluid.

Here as I wonder whether I'm about to face widowhood before I'm thirty years old.

Here, here, here in this place, in this situation,

I am to worship."

Hannah made this same decision. She chose to leave her worries at the temple with a God who could actually handle them. She chose to get up from her weeping, set her course, change her behavior, and change her countenance. Hannah was transformed not because of what God had done in her *situation*, but because of what He had accomplished in her *heart*.

And the next morning, she worshipped.

Flip to the table of contents, and you'll notice that the title for this chapter is "Woman of Waiting." As an act of worship, I want you to cross out the word *Waiting* and retitle the chapter "Woman of Worship." We will eventually see that Hannah worshipped God multiple times and in multiple ways in the short biblical narrative about her life. But this occurrence recorded in 1 Samuel 1:19 is one of the most beautiful—and she does not yet have what she longs for.

One of the most touching sacrifices of praise that we can give to God is to worship Him, to declare Him worthy *while we wait*. He is worthy to be worshipped whether or not we ever get our way! If worship is defined as giving homage, reverence, respect, admiration, devotion, or tribute to someone, then—whether we feel like it or not—He is worthy of that worship even in our moments of waiting.

Look up Habakkuk 3:17–19. What is the situation in these verses?

But what does the author of Habakkuk 3:17–19 choose to do?

Use your imagination. What character traits of God do you think enabled Hannah to turn from her weeping and enter into worship while she waited on Him?

Check out Psalm 145, especially verses 13b–21. Write down some attributes of God that remind you that He is worthy.

Write a prayer telling God how worthy He is of your worship. If necessary, confess that you have not treated Him as such during your season of want or waiting.

Prayer Time for a Woman of Waiting

Ask God for the strength to rise from your place of weeping, change your countenance, change your behavior, and worship Him as He deserves.

Thank God for who He is, not for what He does. Be specific as you bring adoration to His throne for His many flawless attributes.

Life Lessons from Hannah

Woman of Wealth
Part 1

Hannah became pregnant.
—1 Samuel 1:20 NIV

Before I Begin, You Must Begin

The Bible passage for this Life Lesson is 1 Samuel 1:19b–20. Read it in your own Bible or here:

> And Elkanah knew Hannah his wife, and the Lord remembered her. And in due time Hannah conceived and bore a son, and she called his name Samuel for she said, "I have asked for him from the Lord."

Does anything stand out to you in today's passage?

This is the chapter where we get to study the part of the story that is everyone's favorite! People always like happy endings. We tend to enjoy the part of the story where the loose ends get tied up, the tenseness is resolved, the hero saves the day, and everyone lives happily ever after. I want you to see how Hannah's true story ended. I want you to see the richness of her journey. I call her a Woman of Wealth.

But before we can discuss Hannah's wealth, we have to get one thing straight. Hannah did get exactly what she prayed for, but nowhere in scripture are we promised that the secret to getting what we want is just praying, pouring out our hearts, and then waiting for God to show up like Santa Claus. That kind of thinking is not scriptural, so I refuse to write a Bible study that would lead you to that conclusion. If you only ever read the account of Hannah, I suppose you could easily draw that mistaken conclusion. That's why it is so important as we study God's Word that we study *all* of it.

Anyone who teaches you that God is up in heaven, waiting to give us what we ask for like a giant candy dispenser, is not being true to the whole counsel of God's Word. So before we study Hannah's wealth, we need to look at some biblical examples of people who did *not* get what they wanted. Remember, God is still worthy of our worship, no matter how our story ends.

Read 2 Samuel 12:7–10, 13–18. (Yeah, that's Second Samuel this time. Don't get confused.) What was David's situation in this passage?

Did David pray for God to intervene in his situation?

Did God answer the way David wanted Him to answer?

Continue reading this account in 2 Samuel 12:19–20. What was David's response when God didn't do things as he had requested?

It might be easy to say that God didn't do what David had requested because this entire horrible situation was brought about by David's sin. So I'll give you another example that illustrates the truth that uttering heartfelt prayers does not guarantee that we will always get what we want. Read what Paul says in 2 Corinthians 12:7–10.

What was Paul's situation in these verses?

Did Paul ask God to intervene in his situation?

Did God answer the way that Paul wanted Him to answer?

What was Paul's response when God didn't do what he asked Him to do?

In my family, we have experienced that sometimes God answers our requests by providing what we ask of Him, but at other times God says no to some of our earnest prayers.

When my husband was sick, thousands of people joined me in praying for instant, unmistakable healing with no waiting and no aftereffects. I reminded God often that I would give Him all the credit if, one glorious day, God would enable us to walk into a doctor's appointment to find absolute confusion because the scans and blood work showed complete health.

Instead, God allowed us to suffer, and wonder, and depend on Him for twenty-one months, not knowing what would happen. God allowed Wayne to lose lymph nodes, a kidney, part of his liver and lungs, and enough other body parts to keep him constantly reminded that he is here on borrowed time. But partially because of that testimony, Wayne is able to speak to teenagers, prisoners, pastors, addicts, churchgoers, and the homeless by telling them his story of how God rescues.

Another prayer request of mine that God did *not* fulfill according to my plan was my dream of mothering a minivan full of children.

Instead, God has allowed us to grieve the loss of our dream of having more biological children so that He could show us the miraculous world of earthly adoption, thereby showing us more and more clearly the depths of His own intentional, pursuing love for us. (See appendix.)

So as we study the concept of Hannah's wealth, please do not hear this author saying, "Pray and get your way." The truth is that when we truly spend time pouring out our hearts before the Lord, truly let God redefine our perspective, truly allow God to change our behavior and our countenance ... that's when we begin to understand that *whatever* God chooses to give us is a blessing.

The growth that comes from loss is a blessing. The compassion that comes from grief is a blessing. To be acquainted with Christ in His suffering is a blessing whether or not we ever get our way. Time spent with our God in sorrow is never wasted, and it's precious no matter how each person's story ends.

Write a prayer about your own personal situation, telling God how much you trust Him. Use David's example of worshipping even when God said no, and use Paul's example of delighting in his weakness. Apply your efforts to making much of God, no matter what your circumstances are.

Now that we know that God is not required to say yes to us, let's look at how Hannah became a Woman of Wealth. *Webster's New World College Dictionary* defines *wealth* as "a large amount (of something) ... valuable products, contents, or derivatives." To be wealthy is to be "rich or abundant (in something specified)."[13]

What attitude in 1 Samuel 1:19a could be considered an aspect of wealth that Hannah obtained?

According to 1 Samuel 1:19b–20a, did Hannah get what she asked for?

Hannah was entrusted with a highly valuable stewardship opportunity in 1 Samuel 1:20. What could define Hannah as a Woman of Wealth in this verse?

To whom did Hannah give the credit for her newfound wealth?

Now, please notice: the word in verse 19 saying that God "remembered" Hannah does not mean that the Almighty had forgotten her. It actually indicates the way we pay special attention to someone or lavish special care upon him or her. In *The Expositor's Bible Commentary*, Ronald F. Youngblood writes that the same Hebrew verb is used in Psalm 8:4, translated as "are mindful of."[14] Read Psalm 8 to understand

---

[13] *Webster's New World College Dictionary*, 4th ed. (2001), s.v. "wealthy."
[14] In Gaebelein, 3:573.

the context of *remembered*. What was the psalmist's response to the realization that God is mindful of him or has remembered him?

According to Romans 5:1–5, what wealth or value (spiritual qualities) can we obtain even in our suffering?

Look up Philippians 3:7–11. Did Paul, writing this letter while in prison, consider himself wealthy?

According to Philippians 3:12–16, what thing of value was Paul striving toward?

In what ways has God already poured out His blessing on you? Write a prayer thanking Him for the ways He has lavished special care upon you. And don't forget: no matter what your situation, no one deserves to breathe or deserves His forgiveness. Every single thing we take for granted each day is an outpouring of God's attention. That's a great place to start your prayer!

Prayer Time for a Woman of Wealth

Ask God to give you a perspective that considers suffering, unanswered prayer, and spiritual growth to be of great value and wealth.

Thank God that He is always working to accomplish His own eternal purposes in your life (Philippians 2:5, 12–18).

Life Lessons from Hannah

Woman of Her Word

...only may the Lord make good his word.
—1 Samuel 1:23 NIV

Before I Begin, You Must Begin

The Bible passage for this Life Lesson is from 1 Samuel 1:21–25. Read it in your own Bible or here:

> When her husband Elkanah went up with all his family to offer the annual sacrifice to the Lord and to fulfill his vow, Hannah did not go. She said to her husband, "After the boy is weaned, I will take him and present him before the Lord, and he will live there always."
>
> "Do what seems best to you," her husband Elkanah told her. "Stay here until you have weaned him; only may the Lord make good his word." So the woman stayed at home and nursed her son until she had weaned him.
>
> After he was weaned, she took the boy with her, young as he was, along with a three-year-old bull, an ephah of flour and a skin of wine, and brought him to the house of the Lord at Shiloh. When the bull had been sacrificed, they brought the boy to Eli. (NIV)

What has already touched your heart from reading this portion of scripture?

In the chapter titled "Woman of Worth," we studied Proverbs 31:10–12. Reread it and summarize it here.

What vow did Hannah make in 1 Samuel 1:11?

What request did Hannah make of Elkanah in 1 Samuel 1:22?

How did Elkanah respond to her request in 1 Samuel 1:23?

Notice what Elkanah did in 1 Samuel 1:21, at the end of the verse.

Do you think it was important to Elkanah that the members of his family keep their word?

The specifics of the vow Elkanah made in 1 Samuel 1:21 were not recorded. According to Ronald F. Youngblood, it is possible that he made a second vow in support of Hannah's vow (1:11) or that this is an unrelated vow.[15] Regardless, as the head of the family, Elkanah bore the responsibility of ensuring that Hannah kept her vow. Read

---

[15] In Gaebelein, 3:574.

Numbers 30:10–15 to get an understanding of the responsibility that weighed on Elkanah's shoulders.

What did Hannah do in 1 Samuel 1:24–25?

It is important to understand that Hannah's plea in 1 Samuel 1:11 was not a rash promise that she later regretted. It was an intentional commitment, and when it came time to keep that promise, she did so joyfully and willingly.

Author Robert D. Bergen writes, "Hannah was a pious woman who profoundly believed that God was powerful and good. She had suffered humiliation and insult for years due to her childlessness, and was pleading with God to give her a child. Her offer was far superior to that of pagans in the region, who might offer to sacrifice a child as a macabre gift to their deity (2 Kings 17:17). Hannah offered to give the son she requested as a living sacrifice, dedicating his life-long service to the Lord."[16]

Sometimes, in the heat of a moment or during a season of total desperation, we turn to God and say, "Just do this for me" or "Just get me out of this situation and *then* I'll give my life to you. I'll go be a missionary, foster that needy child, go to Bible college, serve at the homeless shelter," and so on.

Have you ever made a promise to God about some act of service you would do for Him or some act of self-denial you were willing to give up for His glory?

---

[16] In Cabal, 407–408.

What does Ecclesiastes 5:1–7 teach us about approaching God?

What does Jesus say about "counting the cost" in Luke 14:28? Read the surrounding verses (25–34) and summarize what Jesus is teaching us about making commitments.

Write a prayer asking God to help you approach Him with all the reverence and holiness that He deserves. Acknowledge your dependence on Him for the strength you will need to keep the commitments you have made to Him.

Prayer Time for a Woman of Her Word

Ask God for a new awareness of what you are saying and promising (Psalm 19:14).

Thank God that He is a faithful, covenant-keeping God (Deuteronomy 7:9, James 1:17–18).

Life Lessons from Hannah

Woman of Wealth
Part 2

And the Lord was gracious to Hannah....
—1 Samuel 2:21a NIV

Before I Begin, You Must Begin

The Bible passage for this Life Lesson is from 1 Samuel 1:20 and 1 Samuel 2:11 and 18–21:

> And in due time Hannah conceived and bore a son, and she called his name Samuel for she said, "I have asked for him from the Lord."
>
> *****
>
> Then Elkanah went home to Ramah. And the boy was ministering to the Lord in the presence of Eli the priest.
>
> *****
>
> Samuel was ministering before the Lord, a boy clothed with a linen ephod. And his mother used to make for him a little robe and take it to him each year when she went up with her husband to offer the yearly sacrifice. Then Eli would bless Elkanah and his wife, and say, "May the Lord give you children by this woman for the petition she asked of the Lord." So they would return to their home. Indeed the Lord visited Hannah, and she conceived and bore three sons and two daughters. And the boy Samuel grew up in the presence of the Lord.

What has God taught you already from the reading of His Word?

In "Woman of Wealth, Part 1," we discussed the fact that Hannah received exactly what she asked God to give her, but that there is no guarantee that it will always happen that way. Through the Old Testament example of David and the New Testament example of Paul, we were challenged to recognize that God often develops in us areas of maturity and spiritual growth as a result of our seasons of suffering, loss, waiting, and prayer. These stand on their own as evidences of God pouring out wealth on us.

We also saw in "Woman of Weeping" that before Hannah had any evidence that she would ever get what she had asked of God, she had already offered that precious gift back to God. In our last chapter, "Woman of Her Word," we saw that Hannah joyfully kept that promise.

Often, the kiddie picture page in Sunday school boils Hannah's story down to this: she wanted a baby, she prayed, God gave her a baby, and she gave the baby back to God—and that covers the basics. But if we end with her presentation of Samuel, we have missed much of God's goodness in Hannah's story.

Please don't misunderstand me. This woman's sacrifice was huge! The surrender of our emotions, hopes, and dreams to God is a precious and important part of the journey. But if we think that we are supposed to dump all these things out before God just so He can take back whatever matters most to us, then we have the wrong picture of God. God is a *giver*, not a *taker*!

Yes, true devotion to Him will require the sacrifice of what matters most to us. Actually it will cost us everything, but in the process of dying to self and identifying with Him, what matters most to us is replaced by what matters most to Him. Only God knows how this transaction works, but in His goodness—in this supernatural trade-off—we make out the best! We become truly wealthy, having been given exactly what we deeply need from the hand of our all-knowing, all-powerful, always-loving Father.

Let's look at how Hannah became a Woman of Wealth.

Hannah's First Sign of Wealth

Check out 1 Samuel 1:20. What is the first evidence of God "remembering" Hannah by lavishing special favor on her?

Hannah's Second Sign of Wealth

Read 1 Samuel 2:20–21a. (We are now in chapter 2 of 1 Samuel, after spending a long time in the first chapter. But isn't God just as concerned about the process as He is the ending?)

What evidence do these verses give of God "remembering" Hannah by lavishing special favor on her?

I love the fact that Eli clarified that he wasn't just praying for Elkanah to have more children through any means necessary. He specified "by this woman" as if to make sure Elkanah knew that Hannah's conception was not a one-and-done miracle. In the eternal economy, the account of Hannah is much more than just "Hannah had her baby, God wanted it back, and that's all she was good for." Eli prayed that Elkanah and Hannah would have more children, and they did. Five more, in fact. And, I would argue, she never really lost Samuel.

The NIV translates Eli's blessing in 1 Samuel 2:20 this way: "May the Lord give you children by this woman *to take the place of the one she prayed for* and gave to the Lord." (Italics added.)

The ESV translates the same blessing this way: "May the Lord give you children by this woman *for the petition* she asked of the Lord." (Italics added.)

According to the Interlinear Bible, the translation goes like this:

"Jehovah shall give you seed of this woman, *because of the prayer she prayed* to Jehovah."[17] (Italics added.)

Do you see any difference in these translations?

Hannah did not lose Samuel; instead, she experienced the unique privilege of being mother to a great prophet. In addition to this honor—and multiplied far beyond the one child for which she had begged God—Hannah also received five more little hearts to influence.

Hannah's Third Sign of Wealth

Read 1 Samuel 2:18–19 and then skip to the end of verse 21, focusing on what was happening with Samuel, not his siblings.

Where and how did Samuel grow up?

---

17 Green, 239.

Now read 1 Samuel 2:11. What was Samuel's job?

Hannah got to watch her child, her surrendered sacrifice, grow up loving and serving the Lord. We would consider this to be "wealth" only if what is important to God is important to us. But considering what we know of Hannah, I believe this was incredibly important to her. Her son became a mighty man of God whose influence over God's people spans two books of the Bible, 1 and 2 Samuel.

If you wonder what became of Samuel, read Psalm 99:5–6. What kind of person did Hannah's boy become? Don't look only at his occupation; look at the end of verse 6 to see the kind of reputation Samuel had.

In Israel's history, Samuel was known for his role as intercessor. He was associated with David in establishing the office of gatekeeper, and he led the Israelites in observing Passover. Known as the first prophet of Israel, he is listed in Hebrews in the great "Hall of Faith." (See Jeremiah 15:1, 1 Chronicles 9:22, 2 Chronicles 35:18, Acts 3:24, Acts 13:20, and Hebrews 11:32.)[18]

This is the legacy that Samuel left behind, a legacy that began with Hannah's surrender. Hannah recognized a truth that David later put into words in Psalm 24:1: "The earth is the Lord's and the fullness thereof, the world and those who dwell therein."

David lived out this truth in 1 Chronicles 29:10–14. According to verse 12, where does all wealth and honor come from?

---

[18] Bromley, 4:312.

When we have the privilege of giving something back to God, we must be mindful that it originally came from His hand (verse 14).

In what ways has God poured out His wealth on you?

Maybe you feel like you have given up something really valuable for God. When your sacrifice comes from a heart of humility like Hannah's, His desire is to give it back to you, purified, pressed down, and overflowing!

Write a prayer thanking Him for his graciousness in your life.

Prayer Time for a Woman of *Abundant* Wealth

Ask God to make you acutely aware of—and grateful for—all the wealth He has poured out on you. Remember from "Woman of Wealth, Part 1" that wealth is not limited to material abundance, but is a measure of the things we possess of value, whether seen or unseen.

Thank God for His blessings poured out within and upon you.

Life Lessons from Hannah

Woman of Worship

My heart rejoices in the Lord....
—1 Samuel 2:1 NIV

Before I Begin, You Must Begin

The Bible passage for this Life Lesson is from 1 Samuel 1:20, 25–28 and 1 Samuel 2:1–10. Read it in your own Bible or here:

1 Samuel 1:20

And in due time Hannah conceived and bore a son, and she called his name Samuel for she said, "I have asked for him from the Lord."

1 Samuel 1:25–28

Then they slaughtered the bull, and they brought the child to Eli. And she said, "Oh, my lord! As you live, my lord, I am the woman who was standing here in your presence, praying to the Lord. For this child I prayed, and the Lord has granted me my petition that I made to him. Therefore I have lent him to the Lord. As long as he lives, he is lent to the Lord." And he worshipped the Lord there.

1 Samuel 2:1–10

And Hannah prayed and said,
"My heart exults in the Lord;
my horn is exalted in the Lord.
My mouth derides my enemies,
because I rejoice in your salvation.
There is none holy like the Lord:
for there is none besides you;

there is no rock like our God.
Talk no more so very proudly,
let not arrogance come from your mouth;
for the Lord is a God of knowledge,
and by him actions are weighed.
The bows of the mighty are broken,
but the feeble bind on strength.
Those who were full have hired themselves out for
bread,
but those who were hungry have ceased to hunger.
The barren has borne seven,
but she who has many children is forlorn.
The Lord kills and brings to life;
he brings down to Sheol and raises up.
The Lord makes poor and makes rich;
he brings low and he exalts.
He raises up the poor from the dust;
he lifts the needy from the ash heap
to make them sit with princes
and inherit a seat of honor.
For the pillars of the earth are the Lord's,
and on them he has set the world.
He will guard the feet of his faithful ones,
but the wicked shall be cut off in darkness,
for not by might shall a man prevail.
The adversaries of the Lord shall be broken to pieces;
against them he will thunder in heaven.
The Lord will judge the ends of the earth;
he will give strength to his king
and exalt the horn of his anointed."

What truths stand out to you in this passage?

Throughout this Bible study, we have been studying Hannah as a Woman of Worship. We have already recognized that our worship of God must not wait until the end of the story. We don't worship Him only when the last curtain falls, the loose ends are tied up, we get our way, or everything is going right. My own definition of worship is to "ascribe worth to." In other words, it is to attribute or give to someone the value he or she is due.

Hannah was worshipping when she poured out her heart to God. She was showing Him that He was worth being presented with her deepest emotions and longing.

Hannah was worshipping when she waited in 1 Samuel 1:19. In these verses, she allowed God to change her outlook and behavior, and she chose to worship while waiting to see what He would do on her behalf.

These are valuable forms of worship, and I would dare say that worship that comes out of these types of situations—the ones that remain unpleasant or unsolved—may be even *more* valuable to God than worship that stems from our abundance.

Nevertheless, when things are going well, we need to give God the worth that He is due. He is always worthy, even though it's a little easier to see and declare it when things are pleasant.

Together, we're going to explore four more ways that Hannah modeled being a Woman of Worship.

First Model of Worship

Read 1 Samuel 1:20. This is not the first time I've asked you to read this verse, but this time look at the name Hannah gave her precious baby. What name did she choose?

Why did Hannah choose this name?

If you have access to Bible study materials, look at various interpretations of the name Samuel. (Or simply look at Hannah's reasoning as recorded in 1 Samuel 1:20.) How was the naming of this child a reflection of where Hannah had placed her hope?

Think of how often a mother uses her child's name. She whispers it in evening prayer and calls it out the front door at dinnertime. She chides the child with his full name when he misbehaves, and she breathes it softly over his feverish brow.

Even when a child, like Samuel, does not dwell with his or her mother, a mother cannot help but mention the name of her child every chance she gets.

Whenever Hannah spoke Samuel's name, her friends and neighbors and the people at the worship place in Shiloh knew that this woman was testifying that her request had been heard by God.

Hannah's life story and the purpose of Samuel's life are wrapped up together in the sweet name his mother cooed as she nursed him, wiped the sweat from his dirty face, and gently ministered to his childhood bumps and bruises. In the mundane days of motherhood,

Hannah chose for her child a name that would constantly declare the truth that God hears the prayers of His people.

Read Deuteronomy 6:4–9. How often does God want His people to contemplate and talk about His faithfulness?

List the auditory and visual reminders provided in these verses to focus the heart and mind on what is important to Him.

Now take inventory. Does your home decor, license plate, holiday tradition, or child's name have a "God story"? If so, please write it in the space provided. If not, pray about how you can intentionally add visual and auditory reminders of God's character into your typical daily life.

Second Model of Worship

Read 1 Samuel 1:28. What precious commodity did Hannah present to the Lord in grateful worship?

Don't forget, this was what was most precious to her. Notice the length of time that Hannah's offering covered. According to 1 Samuel 1:28, how long was Hannah's child going to belong to the Lord?

This was Hannah's dream, status symbol, and hope for future provision and security—and she gave it to God! At this point in the biblical narrative, did Hannah know that she was going to have five more children?

This was Hannah's one thing, her "if only." This was the very thing she begged God for, the thing she wanted most, the thing she cried over and prayed for, and she gave it right back to the One who had given it to her.

In the first chapter, I asked you to be honest with yourself and identify your one thing. (Don't get hung up on the fact that Hannah's one thing was a baby. The point is what Hannah *did* with that desire.)

Now, what is the thing you want most? And if you actually got it, what would you do with it? Would you put it right back into God's hands, knowing that you can trust Him with what you value most?

Now that you have studied Hannah's longings and her willingness to surrender them, write a prayer about what God has revealed to you regarding your own longings and your ability to surrender them.

Third Model of Worship

Hannah worshipped through her verbal praise. Read her song/prayer in 1 Samuel 2:1–10.

Do you see what Hannah was doing here? She was declaring to everyone present at Shiloh the attributes of God. She was telling everyone who her God was! Her psalm of praise reveals the depth of her understanding about God.

Take each phrase or verse and write a summary statement in the margin of your Bible declaring who He is. In case you need help, I have included my own list of summary statements, placed here out of order. See if you can place each simple statement alongside the phrase(s) or verse(s) it summarizes.

He is creator.
He is holy.
He is defender.
He is the God who turns things upside down.
He is provider.
He is the God who gives and takes away.
He is the God of life and eternity.
He is her joy.
He is protector.
He is the rock.
He is judge.

He is all this and much more. Hannah was unafraid to tell the world about her God. Are you?

Read a similar prayer of praise voiced by Mary about the birth of her child. What attributes of God does Mary speak about in Luke 1:46–55?

What attribute of God is most precious to you?

On what scripture do you base this belief in who He is?

Write a statement of praise, telling God what you love about who He is. If you're feeling creative, try using the models of Hannah and Mary to form your own praise psalm about God's attributes.

Fourth Model of Worship

Read 1 Samuel 1:26–28. What did Hannah say about herself in verse 26?

I believe one of the most precious ways Hannah worshipped was through her "used to be" testimony. "I *was* the woman who …"

As she came to dedicate Samuel in the house of the Lord, Hannah was no longer defined as she had been in years past. Previously, she had been weeping, unsettled, and refusing to eat, but these evidences of sorrow no longer characterized her demeanor! She was no longer downhearted, nor was her heart "bad" or grudging. She didn't come on this occasion to pour out her heart before the Lord, nor did she need to ask any favor of the Sovereign One.

But neither did she hide the fact that, *yes,* she had once been that woman. It's almost as if Hannah was trying to get Eli to remember the distraught, weeping woman from two or three years earlier.

Hannah didn't have to be that vulnerable. She could have gone to the temple that day and blended unnoticed into the background. She could have sent Samuel to the temple with Elkanah. And although it would have been wrong, she could have kept him at home with her and refused to fulfill her vow.

Hannah was not required to remind Eli of who she had once been, but she chose to do so anyway.

In today's vernacular, it's like she's saying, "Remember me? Remember me, Eli? I was the woman you thought was a drunken spectacle. I was a basket case. I had a deep need, and I poured it out right here in this place. And look at me now! Look what God has done!"

I might be overly dramatizing scripture, but the important thing is that Hannah was unafraid to "fess up" to who she used to be. She made no attempt to try to make herself look more spiritual or more put together than she truly was.

What was Hannah's motivation in sharing this piece of her story? Read 1 Samuel 1:27 and write down what Hannah ultimately wanted those around her to focus on.

Hannah allowed God to get the glory He deserved for transforming her into the woman she was on that day.

Why are we so afraid to tell our stories?

Author Nancy Leigh DeMoss says, "Many [Christian women] are in bondage to their past. Whether the result of their own failures or the failures of others, their pasts hang like huge weights around their necks—they carry them everywhere they go, trudging through life."[19]

But I want to tell you today that whoever you once were is part of the glory God gets for transforming you into who are you today. Humble yourself. Tell your story!

---

[19] DeMoss, 17.

Maybe your story will be told on stage or social media. Maybe you need to tell it to your small group, or just to one woman whom God is leading you to mentor. Maybe that one woman is your daughter.

My own interest in the biblical account of Hannah began because someone was willing to share her "used to be" story with me. And the "Samuel" in this woman's story ... was me.

I grew up knowing that my mother had a condition called placenta previa when she was pregnant with me. The doctor placed her on bedrest for the two months before my birth. It was a risky time for her as the baby inside continued to grow to full term. It was a time of waiting, a time full of prayer, worry, and study of the Word.

When I was born safely, my mother sent out my birth announcements with 1 Samuel 1:27 written on them, "For this child I prayed, and the Lord has granted me my petition that I made to him." She also wrote my name and birth date next to that verse in her Bible.

That was the story I had always heard growing up, so I was surprised to hear more of the story just before my graduation from high school. Shortly after I had started attending that small, private Christian school, my mom had started working there. During senior chapel, she was asked to give a parent testimony, and she told the entire high school the story that I just told you.

But then she surprised me. With tears in her eyes and her voice slightly wavering, she said, "But when Karen was born, I refused to write 1 Samuel 1:28 on Karen's birth announcements. That verse says, 'Therefore I have lent him to the Lord. As long as he lives, he is lent to the Lord.'"

My mother continued, "I didn't *want* to give Karen back to the Lord. I had prayed so hard just to have her arrive safely, and I just knew that if I gave her back to the Lord, she would end up being a missionary in Africa or something. But now I know that there is no better place for Karen to be than in God's will. I want her to be happy, and I know she can't truly be happy unless she is in the center of His will. So I am here today to say now what I *would not say* when she was born: "Therefore, I have lent her to the Lord. As long as she lives, she belongs to the Lord.'"[20]

Let me tell you, to a seventeen-year-old sitting in senior chapel, those words were powerful. My life was not my own.

That chapel day was the beginning of my interest in the biblical, historical person of Hannah. My interest turned into personal study that became the basis for a speech presented in college, and then developed into speaking sessions for women's retreats. And now it is published in this book with the hope that it will reach the hearts of many more women and affect them as deeply as it has affected me.

But it was all made possible because my mother was willing to tell her story, a story that began with, "I once was the woman who ..."

My mom did not hide the unflattering pieces of her internal struggle. She did not try to make herself appear more spiritual in front of my classmates and her coworkers. She did not try to stop the tears that flowed down her cheeks as she told the story of what God had done in her life and the transformation He had accomplished in her heart.

What about you? Has God answered your prayers? Has He changed your situation? More importantly, has He changed your heart? Has He brought you to a place where you can worship Him even while you are waiting? Take a moment to jot down your "used to be" story on the next page.

---

[20] Van Cott.

Journal Space

Look back at the previous page and reflect on the story God has given you. God gave you that story to be used for His glory, but that involves a balance that is hard for many women.

There is a fine line between *telling* our story for the sake of attention and self-glorification, and *hiding* our story for the same reasons. When we refuse to share our story in appropriate ways, we attempt to steal from God some of the glory He deserves for transforming us into who we are today by His grace.

Hannah gave us a beautiful example of how to tell our story. Read 1 Samuel 1:26 through 2:10. How many verses in this passage reflect on who Hannah previously was?

How many verses reflect on what God did for Hannah?

How many verses reflect on what Hannah did for God?

How many verses call the hearers to contemplate the truth about who God is?

What is God asking you to do with your testimony? What is your inclination when left on your own? Do you try to hide your "used to be" story? Do you tell it often and loudly to make much of yourself, or like Hannah are you willing to share it when it is appropriate? Is your goal to honestly say who you once were so that you may use most of your time and energy pointing people to the truth about what God has done and who He is?

Pray and ask God for opportunities to tell your story for His glory.

After praying, take some time to write out your story using Hannah's model as an example. This should be a revision of your first "used to be" story, with more emphasis on the unchanging character of God.

Prayer Time for a Woman of Worship

Ask God for a pure heart with which to worship Him, ideas for surrounding yourself with auditory and visual reminders of His goodness, opportunities to declare His character, and a willingness to share your story for His glory in appropriate ways and at appropriate times.

Thank God for the miracles He has performed in your heart and life. Praise Him that He is worthy to be worshipped no matter how your story ends.

Afterword

[Day 24]

Hannah's "used to be" story is one of potential embarrassment, but she revealed it anyway to make much of God. How is Paul's "used to be" story in Philippians 3:4–6 different from Hannah's?

According to Philippians 3:7–10, what is Paul's response to his own pedigree?

Where is the focus for both Hannah and Paul?

As you reflect on your own story, read Galatians 2:20. As believers, where does our identity rest?

Read 1 Samuel 2:10. Hannah's words about a king or anointed one have caused some people to consider her a prophetess.[21] This is the first Old Testament reference to someone being "the anointed one." There may be no warranted connection between this anointed one and Jesus, the Messiah, but the value of the content found in

---

[21] Cabal, 408–409.

114

Hannah's psalm of praise is so stirring that many believe Mary used it as a model in her own Magnificat, spoken in praise at the birth of *the* Anointed One.[22]

The name Hannah appears in the Old Testament only in 1 Samuel 1 and 2, the chapters we have just finished studying. However, the New Testament reveals another prophetess named Hannah in Luke 2:36–38. Unfortunately, the incorrect spelling in the King James Version ("Anna") has become accepted.[23] In this New Testament passage, to whom does Anna/Hannah give honor?

Read John 6:38 and John 17:1–5. Who did Jesus say that He came to earth to glorify?

Read Philippians 1:21. How does Paul view death in this verse?

Why does Paul view death this way? (See Philippians 1:23)

Now go back to Philippians 1:21. According to Paul's view, what is the purpose of his life?

---

[22] Walvoord, 434.

[23] Gaebelein, 3:575.

From beginning to end, scripture presents us with a God who is worthy of our worship. The life each of us has been given is simply a tool in our hands to offer up in worship of Him.

Write a prayer, offering God all that you have and all that your story consists of, asking Him to use it to bring glory to Himself.

Becoming a Woman of Worship begins when we ...

surrender our wants to Him ...

> and find that He is enough,

define our worth in Him ...

> and find that our value comes neither
> from what we have nor from what we lack,

take our wounds to Him ...

> and find that He is the healer,

weep in His presence ...

> and find that He is the comforter,

and wait in the shelter of His wings ...

> and find Him to be our refuge.

When we worship Him
simply because He is worthy,
we find that He pours out
wealth upon wealth
onto us.

Psalm 145

I will exalt you, my God the King;
I will praise your name for ever and ever.
Every day I will praise you
and extol your name for ever and ever.
Great is the Lord and most worthy of praise;
his greatness no one can fathom.
One generation commends your works to another;
they will tell of your mighty acts.

They will speak of the glorious splendor of your majesty—
and I will meditate on your wonderful works.
They will tell of the power of your awesome works—
and I will proclaim your great deeds.
They will celebrate your abundant goodness
and joyfully sing of your righteousness.
The Lord is gracious and compassionate,
slow to anger and rich in love.
The Lord is good to all;
he has compassion on all he has made.

All you have made will praise you, O Lord;
your saints will extol you.
They will tell of the glory of your kingdom
and speak of your might,
so that all men may know of your mighty acts
and the glorious splendor of your kingdom.
Your kingdom is an everlasting kingdom,
and your dominion endures through all generations.

The Lord is faithful to all his promises
and loving toward all he has made.
The Lord upholds all those who fall

and lifts up all who are bowed down.
The eyes of all look to you,
and you give them their food at the proper time.
You open your hand
and satisfy the desires of every living thing.

The Lord is righteous in all his ways
and loving toward all he has made.
The Lord is near to all who call on him,
to all who call on him in truth.
He fulfills the desires of those who fear him;
he hears their cry and saves them.
The Lord watches over all who love him,
but all the wicked he will destroy.
My mouth will speak in praise of the Lord.
Let every creature praise his holy name
for ever and ever.

(NIV, italics added)

Appendix

The topic of adoption was broached in "Woman of Wealth, Part 1." For further study on the miraculous concept of spiritual adoption and redefined identity, consider the truths found in the following verses:

Romans 8:12–17

Galatians 4:4–7

1 John 3:1–3

1 Peter 2:9–10

Colossians 1:9–14

1 Corinthians 6:9–11

Bibliography

Bromley, Geoffrey W., ed. *The International Standard Bible Encyclopedia*. 4 vols. Grand Rapids, MI: Eerdmans, 1988.

Cabal, Ted, ed. *The Apologetics Study Bible*. Nashville, TN: Holman Bible, 2007.

DeMoss, Nancy Leigh. *Lies Women Believe and the Truth that Sets Them Free*. Chicago, IL: Moody, 2001.

Dyrli, Karl. "Fame and Glory." Sermon presented at Sunday morning worship service. Fellowship Evangelical Free Church, Dallas, PA. January 1, 2017.

Gaebelein, Frank E., ed. *The Expositor's Bible Commentary*. 12 vols. Grand Rapids, MI: Zondervan, 1992.

Green, Jay P. *The Interlinear Bible: Hebrew-Greek-English*. Peabody, MA: Hendrickson, 1986.

Hughes, Tim. "Here I Am to Worship." 2001.

Kaiser, Walter C. Jr., Peter H. Davids, F. F. Bruce, and Manfred T. Brauch. *Hard Sayings of the Bible*. Downers Grove, IL: InterVarsity, 1996.

Kaiser, Walter C. Jr., and Duane Garrett, eds. *NIV Archaeological Study Bible*. Grand Rapids, MI: Zondervan, 2005.

Ramirez, Marc. "A Call to Consecration." Sermon presented at Sunday morning worship service. Fellowship Evangelical Free Church, Dallas, PA. January 29, 2017.

Van Cott, Carlene. April 2017. Personal communication. Used by permission.

Vos, Howard F. *Nelson's New Illustrated Bible Manners and Customs*. Nashville, TN: Thomas Nelson, 1999.

Walvoord, John F., and Roy B. Zuck. *The Bible Knowledge Commentary: Old Testament*. Victor Books, 1985.

Acknowledgments

A person does not successfully write and publish a book without the investment of many significant people around her.

Always and utmost, all glory belongs to Christ my King. Without Him, I can do nothing. With Him, I can do everything He has called me to do (John 15:4–5).

Tremendous thanks goes to Pastor Dwight Hodne for proofreading this book for theological content. Thank you so much for offering your time and for providing personal comments, insights, thought provoking questions, and additional Scripture on which to meditate.

I am also indebted to Holly Hodne for being willing to proofread along with her husband, offering me insight on the appeal of this study to a broad range of women, the feasibility of the exercises, and opportunities for gospel presentation throughout this Old Testament narrative. Holly, I absolutely loved reading your personal comments throughout the "notebook version" of the study. Thank you for sharing your personal experiences and feelings with me. I desperately wanted a proofreading *team* for this book project, and I was so blessed when I got that team in the two of you. Lauren was right when she said she knew the perfect couple for the job!

I am grateful to Mrs. Charlotte Upchurch, my college speech professor, for assigning a task that found its ultimate completion in this book.

Thank you to the amazing team of women who created such a beautiful cover. You have skills that I do not possess, and I am amazed by you. I am honored to call you my friends, and I am richer for the gifts you each bring to the table:

Sara Wise, you are the most beautiful cover model I've ever seen, and you embody the heart of a Woman of Worship.

Leeann Manzoni, your photography skills amaze me. Thank you for taking the time to capture just the right atmosphere in Sara's photo. I will always cherish the special day we spent doing the photo shoot down by the creek, along with Sara, Querida, Taylor, and Joshua.

Melissa Vosburgh, you are a faithful friend. Thank you for loving me just as I am, and yet making me look like a professional author. How do you do it?

Lauren Hodne, I am without words. (Shocking, I know.) I simply drew a stick figure and scribbled some words on a sheet of copy paper, and you designed the cover to look like *this*. You made my vision a reality. I love it!

My gratitude goes out to all who have encouraged and supported me along the way, waiting with expectant hope and believing that this book would one day be in print:

Joan Werzinski, thank you for always asking how my book was coming. I know it took a long time to bring it to completion, but you have no idea how much those simple comments encouraged me to pursue this God-given calling.

Carolyn Trosky, thank you for investing in me and for taking the time to mentor me. Thank you for helping me begin to understand Psalm

46:10, "Be still and know that I am God." Thank you for affirming my gift. It means more than you know.

Melissa Ferrari, thank you for walking a mile with me. The journey is always made sweeter when I share it with you. Like the disciples on the road to Emmaus, we enjoy traveling together, and yet the real value of the time we share is only realized when we recognize that we have been in *His* presence (Luke 24).

Paul and Cheryl Jackson, your consistent prayers, support, inquiries, and encouragement have been a treasure to me.

Leisa Campbell, thank you for being willing to receive random text messages about clunky sentences and other crises in need of a grammar cop. My finished work is better because of you, and you will be glad to know that I take full responsibility for all remaining errors. I either didn't ask you about them or ignored your excellent advice.

Thank you to my personal prayer team. You are now seeing just one evidence of the labor that is accomplished by your time on your knees. There is much more fruit than just this book, but most of it is harder to see than a book that can be held in one's hand. I thank you for each and every one of those fruits. You bear my burdens just as the friends of the paralytic carried him in his moments of weakness, *and you bring me to Jesus* (Mark 2:1–12). That is all I could ever ask.

Thank you to Joshua, who loaned me a quiet place to work at his desk while I finished this book in peace.

Thank you to my parents, who have always supported my writing endeavors and have prayed and encouraged this book project.

Mom, *this* is the book I always thought I would write first, the book that has been on my heart since college. I always thought that when I wrote this book, I would dedicate it to you. You always believed that God would use me to write a book—and such a huge part of the catalyst for *this* book was your own personal story. But God had other plans, and He led me on another journey where *He* wrote another story, and I obeyed Him by publishing it. I made the decision that you deserved to have my first book dedicated in your honor even if it wasn't the one I thought it would be. I'm fairly sure that you won't mind sharing this book with the person to whom I have chosen to dedicate it. I know you have a rather soft spot in your heart for her, and I am certain that your prayer for her is the same as mine. Thank you, thank you, thank you for telling me your story. Thank you for praying for me. Thank you for allowing me to share this story—*our story*—with others. May God receive all the glory.

To my best friend and greatest champion, thank you for believing in me and in this book. Thank you, Wayne, for valuing my gift enough to encourage me to write, even when I'm willing to let this calling slip to the sidelines underneath the never-ending piles of dirty dishes and laundry. Thank you for doing your best to give me the gift of *peace* in the midst of our crazy schedule and busy household, so that I could focus on bringing this book to completion. Thank you for being like Elkanah and seeing worth in me even when I cannot see it in myself. Thank you for *not* being like Elkanah and never taking a second wife because of my insufficiencies. I super appreciate that about you! "Two are better than one" for a whole bunch of reasons (Ecclesiastes 4), and I am a better *me* because I share my life with *you*.

Thank you, God, for the gift of Your Word and its power to change us from the inside out (Hebrews 4:12).

About the Author

Karen Morgan's first book was *Morgan Update: Please Forward*, the chronicle of her journey alongside her husband as he fought for his life in a severe battle with cancer. She is a devoted wife and loving mother who finds that most of her days are filled with piano lessons, art lessons, and soccer or basketball games. Karen has always loved the Bible, and she holds a bachelor's degree in religious education. She is an advocate for earthly adoption because she cannot get over the intentional, pursuing, on-purpose kind of love that the Heavenly Father has so perfectly demonstrated to her. She loves to teach God's Word to women. She and her family live in Pennsylvania, where they minister to teenagers and ministry families. Check out her website at wayneandkaren.com.

Printed in the United States
By Bookmasters